MW00330002

The bitter taste
of happiness

r.m. pineda

Thank you for the support
and enjoy the read!

Jmpineda

For Francheska.

I fucking did it.

If you find yourself within the words I have written, I hope it brings you at ease.

If you find someone you know within the words I have written, I hope it provides you with transparency.

Happiness is hard work.
There is no real formula for it.
Just a lot of trial and error.

… there's a mathematical
certainty that
someone else is feeling that
exact thing
this is not to say you aren't special
this is to say thank God
you aren't special…

Neil Hilborn

I asked her,
"Why... Why did you do all of this?"

She said,
"I did it to be happy."

She binged on happiness
and became drunk with
spontaneity

- joyful impulses

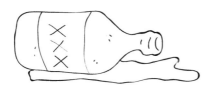

She blossomed
from the bud
that walled her in
as her petals
strew infinitely

- her own type of wallflower

I have all the right reasons
to be happy
and yet
somehow
the only happiness
I have ever known
is now in someone else's
hands

- misplaced happiness

She says she loves him
but when her eyes meet mine, she looks
at me with that same gaze the first time
she said I love you
She says she loves him
but when I look at her, she'll always try to
find me over the horizon of his shoulders
as if I'm the setting sun as she watches me
dip into darkness
She says she loves him
but when she hugs me, she hugs me
tighter than a soldier would coming back
to their family because I know that she's
found her way back home each time
She says she loves him
but every time we talk, it feels like it's
only you and I, where the bullshit around
us just stops for a while as we exchange
the good ole times through our endless
conversations and banter

. . .

She says she loves him
And I know she does... When she talks
about him, she smiles the way she used to
about me
A smile only I can recognize
A smile that we've shared countless times
that I
still get out of her but only when she talks
about him
A smile only I was able to give her
She says she loves him
but I know she still loves me
When I look at her and she looks at me,
we still see ourselves within each other
No force can wipe the homes that we have
built within ourselves
She says she loves him
and I truly am happy for her
but I... I'll always be her person

- her lobster

I'm well.
I'm doing well.
The only darkness I ever dwell in
now is the black coffee that used to
consume me.
I swallow that shit with ease now.

- coffee thoughts I

My heart aches
for not that
she is gone
My heart aches
for it would not
kill her if
I was

- sappy heart

The devil oozes
beneath my sanity
and it is only he
who gives me
hope in finding
solace

- comfortable demise

She found her way over the moon
and without ever looking back
She seized the everlasting
sunshine that shone
across her face

- grimace full of sunshine

I wasn't much of a
dreamer until
I realized
I was living a nightmare
A roller coaster of
endless inceptions
I have grown to accept
that I may be
stuck in this limbo
forever

- good mourning

The moment I saw us growing into
everything we did not aspire to
become, it became evident that I
was blinded by the illusions of love
and got too used to the idea of being
with you

The real battle
is not how you choose
to suppress these nightmares,
it's how you conquer
the demons within,
before they bury you
with them

- 6 feet under consciousness

Despite her hating the taste of
coffee,
her lips tasted more bitter
than a fresh brew
with every spiteful word she said.

- coffee thoughts II

We didn't tend to the garden
we built together and failed to
bloom into everything we
could've potentially been

Nothing good happens after 2am
they say
and so there was one time at 4am
you called me behind his back
because you still found comfort in
me just as much as I did in you

- half conscious spews

As far as I can tell, the only
approval you consider for yourself
is from your impulse and not your
heart

- spur of emotions

I ended it with you so you can
flourish and be all the things you've
always imagined yourself to be
but all you did was put yourself
in the exact
same position
and it's a shame
My love is still there but
it's morphed itself into the
shape of
sympathy

My value came
as an
epiphany after you left
where I realized
I am worth more
than what you left
me to be
and your presence
is no longer what
will suffice for my happiness

- more self-love I

If I could love less then I would
probably be the happiest mother
fucker alive.
I would shamelessly play video
games till 3 am on a nightly basis,
go and hang out with my boys more
often
or maybe even fuck around and
download tinder like all my friends
have been suggesting.
If I could love less then I'd probably
stop caring too much about things
even if they didn't directly impact
me.
My Twitter timeline wouldn't be a
bunch of retweets of quote tweets
of people making a smart or witty
remark about something messed up
Trump may have said or something
stupid Jake Paul may have done
like doxing Post Malone 'cause god
dammit, I love Post Malone.
If I could love less then I would've
probably been saner the last few
months.

She wouldn't have hurt me
as much as she did…
I wouldn't have been
wallowing in my sorrows,
idle under these blankets
hiding the stream of tears
flooding the sheets.
I wouldn't have been going
to work and my coworkers
asking me, "When the hell did
you start taking your coffee black?"
and I say, "Since I found out my
ex moved on fast as fuck
to the dude I should have been
worrying about since she
became friends with him the
last year, right after we
literally broke up,"
cause I've been feeling bitter
as hell.
If I could love less then
I probably wouldn't have shown
her Rick and Morty because that's
my favourite show and every time I
watch it I can't help but imagine her
laugh in the back of my mind.

If I could love less then I
probably wouldn't have cared
too much about how she
always starved herself... so I
taught myself how to cook
Italian food because that's one
of the only things she loved eating.
If I could love less then I don't
think I would have loved her
at all,
and despite the ending she
provided to our story I don't
take it for granted.
Despite her somehow saying
I love you to the guy I should
have been worrying about the
last year after all we've been
through, and to her I say...
thank you.

Thank you for providing me with
clarity.
For knowing the type of love I
deserve.
I wasn't the most perfect boyfriend
but neither were you the most
perfect girlfriend.
If I could love less then I probably
wouldn't have settled with comfort,
but who am I kidding, even if we
broke it off earlier it would have still
resulted in what you did because I
know that if I was able to love any
less than I was capable of, I probably
wouldn't be in this position of being
afraid to love anyone as much as I
have loved you.

- traumatic type of love

I'm trying to learn how to love
black coffee as I'm trying to learn
how to love myself.

- coffee thoughts lll

She says everything is fine but I
know that face
I've read this face too many times
to understand that
everything is not
She is a girl full of adventure and
yet always seems to not be sure
what she is searching for

- misguided happiness

The idea didn't hit me too
hard until
I noticed my heart drop
when I saw your familiar
lips on his.
My mind caught in a frenzy
of emotions
remembering everything
we've done together as
flashes of you and I
projected in my mind
quickly and that I couldn't
help but feel my world go
back to that reality...
I still love you.

. . .

It's been many months since
you've been with him but my heart
stays loyal to your soul but still
destroyed by the way you broke it.
My mind still stained by the
happiness you provided but
still incapable of the idea of you
sharing that happiness with
someone else.
A little more time is all I need I guess.
As I find the remnants of my sanity,
surviving these wild emotional
endeavours, I hope you found
everything you've ever hoped for.

- god damn

As beautiful as the view may be,
my climb will only
leave me reminded
of the paradise
I can never reach.

- idle state of sadness

I've been told
a handful of
times of how
strong of a person
I am.

I think I'm just one hell of an actor.

- a walking paradox

…Life is a gym membership
with a really complicated
cancellation policy…

Rudy Francisco

10 things I have to stop doing in this modern age of crazy that have made me go crazy after we broke up.

1. I gotta stop stalking your twitter and going through your likes to see how your feeling throughout the day just to see if you're thinking about him with all the lovey dovey tweets or bitter about me with all the spiteful tweets about choosing your happiness first or "that love is love or love is spontaneous" tweets.

2. I gotta stop checking the "find my friends" app on our iPhones to see where you are at all times just so I can make sure I know where you are at all times and so that my curiosity isn't driving me crazy to assure that you aren't at his house.

3. Stop questioning myself...

'Cause wait, you are at his house.

4. Swearing.

'Cause fuck why did I check. I had feeling you were there but I checke anyway.

5. I gotta stop liking all you Instagram posts with him so yo wouldn't be aware that I know ho awesome your life seems to be wit him.

6. I gotta stop going through the lis of people who watched my snapcha story to specifically find your nam just so I too can show you ho awesome my life i

7. Stop taking the meticulous thing to heart... because I tried to go on he twitter, Instagram and see if she sav my story just now or know where sh is in this world but can't seem to fin her. She blocked me on everything

8. Stop feeling like the world revolves around me and that only I have problems because of this.

It's not like I was all up on her social media or anything. I didn't accidently like her pic on insta or tweet on twitter did I?!?

The last source of social media I go on is my Facebook. I stopped using Facebook ever since my mom got it but something possessed me to log back onto it and there I see, she hasn't blocked me on it...yet. I know she doesn't really use Facebook either but I see that her profile picture is of her and her new man.
Later on my mom asks me if everything is alright. I tell her, "Yeah. Why?" She asks, "Does she have a new boyfriend?" ...And in that moment I realized that my mom was still friends with her on Facebook.

While caught in a micro stupor she says, "Roger, whatever you're going through, I'll always be here for you." But even I didn't know what I was going through or what the hell I was even trying to achieve through all this other than finding myself going crazy and becoming into a creep. It wasn't until I looked at my mother and realized how privileged we are to know what true love is. Her face said it all...

Understand that in this modern age of love, anything goes. We are blessed to be able to choose who we love. Or that we're just stupid and find ourselves crazy in love.
Whatever the case may be,

. . .

9. Never take this liberty of finding your soulmate for granted because not only is it a privilege to be loved but when this age of modern loves' currents ceased motion, we were able to scour the waters and find the paradise we desired. And although it's taken this amount of time to heal...

10. Stop being stuck in the fucking past and move the fuck on because I know my worth. I'm better than this. No need to cling onto something that is no longer there but rather focus on everything that is. No need to especially lose my sanity by being crazy about you. If you can put me aside just like that, so can I. If you can find your soulmate, I hope I can too.

- the opportunity of loving

I used to have
5 coffees a day
because I felt that I was able to taste
you through the
bitterness
it provided.

- coffee thoughts IV

Yeah, you found someone who makes
you happy, but happiness is
impermanent. As for me,
I found myself.
I found what you have been
striving for all this time and you
rely on another to somehow fulfill,
only to remain wandering in
an infinite spiral of uncertainty.
So the way you feel right now
was at one point something you
felt with me, and through it all,
it doesn't seem too special cause it just
seems like you're simply trying
to relive our good times again.
I know you.
Yeah, you're happy,
but ultimately,
I know you aren't.

- outer realization

I did not realize how
much you held me back
when I later found love in all the
people you told me not to
talk to

The only father I have been
looking up to recently is time

- tick tock

As soon as I hear her voice...
My body tenses up and my train of
thought depletes. I'm lost for words and
remain paralyzed until I'm not.
Her voice strikes a note in me
only she can
sing the melody to.

- musical ingenious

When I looked in the mirror,
I couldn't recognize who was
standing in front of me. When I
looked at you, I didn't recognize
that smile on your face. We were
completely different people before
all this. But when I look at myself
now, I see a familiar face...
one that hasn't smirked genuinely
like that in a long time. When I look
back at you now however, I still see
the same girl drowning in her endless
sorrows behind that deceiving smile.
A smile that slowly weakened and
began shaking more just to try and
hold this false portrayal of happiness.
We left each other's arms to blossom
into the people we once were.

. . .

You were strong and courageous
and positive and enjoyed
everything about life but slowly
disintegrated into a nomad lost
in our past, trying to rekindle
something that is no longer in
reach... and so I wanted you to
find yourself but all you did was
maintain this same demeanour in
the arms of someone else. Maybe
you still don't know what you really
wanted after me... but that's okay.
I found out what I wanted.
What I needed.

- reliving in the new

You're like a politician full of promises,
a privileged colonizer in my mind but
after moving on that fast, I'm like the
indigenous with how you've
neglected our history.
You gave me your love and I fell
drunk in it.
I gave you my soul
but you traded yours
leaving me with nothing
as you stowed away
without having to pay the taxes I did.
Leaving me on a reserve
as my emotions profusely boil.
It's been going on for too long.
I've been fighting one hell of a fight to
know that my freedom is a revolution you
were never able to handle.

- hollow assurance

I love sleep but not enough to
actually try to get a good night sleep
I let the tears drown me out
and the fatigue to wear me down
so I can anticipate what losing myself is
like and won't be afraid to do so
when it happens

She measured my love by
putting value
on how much money
I spent on her

- I feel emptier

You cannot expect
the full satisfaction of
somebody else's love
if you don't even love
yourself

She was a girl full of love
and always seemed to
find it in others
but never for herself

- more self-love II

I had all the love in the world to
give you
but it wasn't the love you wanted
and to be honest,
I'm not sure it's a
love language anyone
can truly interpret

We're just two lonely people
trying to hate ourselves
a little less.

BoJack Horseman

These lips.
These lips, white and chapped.
Dry to the cracks.
Lifeless and held together by the
petroleum jelly that resurrects life
back to it each time.
It holds the 16 tremors that have
shaken for every grey,
lifeless corpse its said farewell to,
buried 6 feet under.
These lips are stained with the
cries of agony, once begging for death
to show them the door and
stop teasing them by letting them
hang off the cliffs of hell as it danced
in the fire.

• • •

These lips still suppress the three
heaviest words at the tip of
its tongue from coming out when
they see her but can never find its way
out because they're still drowning from
the pool of tears it's accumulated.
These lips have encountered the devil
so many times, they don't even flinch
at the sight of a demon
I don't know if it's true but
apparently you use more muscles
when frowning...
And so I've been smiling a little more
lately because I'd like to at least think,
it makes me feel a little less exhausted.

- I guess I really am one hell of
an actor

As she slept at peace every night
and learned to love again
I constantly replayed our memories
like a bad mix tape in trying to find the
reasons why you did such a thing
I don't think I can ever sleep
easy knowing I'm the reason
why someone is hurting deep inside

...my depression is a shape shifter
One day it is as small as a firefly
in the palm of a bear
The next it's the bear
On those days I play dead
until the bear leaves me alone...

Sabrina Benaim

To understand what
living with depression
is like,
breathing feels like
it's the best form
of passive suicide.
It gives me a
glimpse of hell
with every breath I take
and a sense of relief
every time I hold my breath.
It doesn't matter if the sun is out
shining brightly or if the birds
are chirping songs wildly,
all the little things
in life that boosts our moods but
never pay attention to,
never fail to always fail
in having to make you
feel better
at being worse.

• • •

Sometimes you become stuck in
your depressive state
and can't do anything about it
but do nothing,
contemplating of a time
you weren't where you are
in that moment.
Sometimes you can't help but
feel that way until you
don't feel that way.
So inhale the relief and
exhale the hell.

It gets better.

A little bit of heaven shines brightly
through the many gates of opportunity
you open each day.

- just hang in there

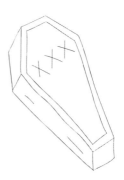

The only time my family
ever has these family reunions is when it's
a funeral.
I've seen the face of death too many times
to know the amount of agony everyone
endures during these periods...
and so I wouldn't want them to have
another family reunion because of me.

- I know the feeling too well

Our greatest downfall wasn't what I could
not give you
It's what you couldn't give yourself
because you let your insecurities eat you
alive
spoiling everything around us

I can only listen to John Mayer's
"slow dancing in a burning room"
so many times to truly remind me
that we really aren't meant to be,
and it's not even that I want to be
back together, but more of a reminder
of how fucked up you left
me to be. And that I fucking love
John Mayer. But even John can't
provide me with the transparency
I'm searching for. Many months later
and I'm still lost in the midst of all
that has transpired.
I don't know who I am.
I feel incomplete.

. . .

The self-declared other half of me is
missing but is now the other half of
another soul whose soul I can feel tickle
mine as the 3rd dimension me is running
out of capacity to truly sustain the
happiness happening on the other side
and is slowly creeping its way into my
sanity.
The worst part is that she knows
I'm hurting.
The worst part is that she knows
I wouldn't ever do this to her.
The worst part is that I'm happy,
she's happy.
And boy, is it so hard to truly
comprehend to myself how I could even
feel that.

- slow dancing in my unfathomable logic

My depressive state has
currently reached its peak,
where no matter
the day of the week,
it feels like a Monday morning
throughout each day,
with a hint of Friday
every two weeks
of Monday mornings.

- what's a Tuesday?

If I had known
I would endure the
same amount of
emotional suffering
leading up to dying again
I don't think I would have
fought so hard the
first time

- never again

In my mind
you remain as the rainbow
refracting in the heaviest of rain
I know I shouldn't
yet I still scour my way
through to the end in hopes of finding the
greatest treasure

I always thought love
brings the best out of someone
but she only ever reminded me of
all the bad things about myself

My emotional numbness has reached
my tongue because I can't even taste the
bitterness I had towards you

- strong distastefulness

We never fought for love
because the love
was always there,
we fought to keep the
house we built from collapsing.

The sad ending you've given me
was the beginning of
the new happiness I have now.

It's hard to embrace someone you aren't
truly proud to be with...
and I'm sorry
it took me a
while to
realize that.

I'm sorry I couldn't change into the
person you wanted me to be, just so you
can be proud of something.

Our love was like a broken home
waiting to fall apart.
I attached the concept of hope
with you and I
for so long that
as I walked out for the first time,
I found hope in the birds freely flying,
the trees naturally swaying with
the wind and through the glimmer of
sunshine seeping through the clouds.
Hope became into an ambiguous world
I wanted to be a part of.

Some things are better off left unsaid, for not everyone has the capacity to handle a truth they are in denial of.

- safe spoke words

The thoughts I'd have if we ever had dinner today.

1. I saw black and white a year ago but am now feeling a little brighter than I was living in your shade.

2. You laugh uncontrollably. You've made me into a punchline I've still yet to laugh at.

3. I freeze when I hear your name. I breathe heavily as I'm brought back to what I endured a year ago.

4. I then go into a mode of me on February 6, 2017. Replaying the exact moment I've learned what it feels like for a heart to break and try to heal itself all in one moment but for the breaking part to continue ensuing, until it reaches your sanity.

5. I remember always feeling like a piece of shit because it was something you were really good at making me feel.

6. I didn't know what depression was until I met you.

7. You still want to be friends with me but you also want me to get used to hearing his name in conversation... I imagine that being the equivalent of walking down an endless hallway of table legs in the shape of squares with all its corners facing my way and placing itself in front of my toes every step I take. Fuck that.

8. I ignored you all these months and you have the audacity to tell me that it hurt you when I did that. Where were you when there were streams of waterfalls running down my face, as I continuously drowned in all the things you loved to tell me about him when we still hung out at first? You knew I still loved you... I don't know if you noticed but that hurt me.

9. I'm not trying to come off as a dick but I mean you came on his dick first.

10. I know this steak tastes bland but with the saltiness I'm feeling in this moment, it tastes heavenly.

11. Despite my bitterness, I hope you're doing well.

12. Remember when you lost that ring I gave you because you were upset at how the necklace I originally gave you didn't have any karats in it? And when you told me you were so sorry that you lost it, I said it was okay? Yeah. It wasn't.

13. I hope you've found everything you were never able to with me.

14. I found me again. I found myself in the company of others. Through the people you told me to stop talking to. Through the people that held me together and helped me pick myself back up, erasing the wall of ideas you wrote across my mind that made me believe that I was no good for anyone.

15. As I figuratively imagine us sitting at that table, I'm glad this dinner is only in my imagination... 'cause god only knows the amount of horror my heart can handle hearing your voice.

- you can breathe now roger.

Love will not
heal me.
But it will
hold my hand
if I ever
heal myself.

Nayo Jones

It's okay to be selfish believe me.
Don't settle for anything less than what
you know you deserve.

I receive a call from an unknown
person, thinking it's my buddy
trying to prank call me and then
I hear a high pitched, "Hi".
She calls me to remind me of
what-could-have-been our
potential 4 years.
After being with a new guy for
8 months, I'm surprised you even
gave a shit about me since
leaving me scarred.
Then she asks, "How are you?"
Well bitch, let me tell you how
the fuck I am.
Since then I've cried my eyes out
for a good 2 months straight,
my grades have dropped,
I have a lot more money saved up,
I've started drinking my coffee black,
I've been able to see my friends that
you dislike so dearly,

. . .

I've done any and everything to forget
your existence,
after reading one self help book
to another,
after playing so much video games
I practically have carpal tunnel syndrome,
after drinking so much till I passed out
multiple times just so I can forget
about you
for a little while,
after listening to enough John Mayer,
after meeting new people and making
friends with people I
would have never met,
and finally receiving this call from you
and hearing your voice...

Better. Doing a lot better now.

- October 15, 2017

And here I am
a year later.
Time has done me well
but I wish I was able to move at her
rate of time.
We are all time travellers
moving at one second per second
but she was able to move at a
rate of one year per forty hours
because she was able to embrace a new
relationship after just
having one for three and a half years.
I've learned to embrace my
sadness and face it
rather than
dwell in it.

- baby steps

The day I looked back and saw
the path I paved for myself,
it made me realize that
no matter what direction I was
coming from,
it was always moving up
towards something uncertain
and so far,
taking those leap of faiths
into darkness enabled me
to recognize that sometimes
the moon is one hell
of a shiny trophy.

Happiness is as impermanent as enduring
sadness because at the end of the day
there is nothing absolute. So keep calm
and allow the currents to guide you to
where you need to be.

- conditional moments

Laugh until you're heart no longer
desires the need to do so
and keep on laughing
because there is nothing more
wonderful than the realization
that your heart is beating
in unison with it.

Nothing good ever comes easy.
It makes me wonder how you
spontaneously found something
so good that easily...
But then I remembered how
easy it was to get you.

- been that way

Through it all, I undoubtedly loved her,
but I wasn't crazy about her.

- lied to myself

This wasn't where I imagined myself to
be but
I'm glad to be here.
I'm thankful to have grown wiser.
I'm thankful to have grown into a person
much greater than I ever thought I could
become.
I'm thankful for you, allowing me to find
a love much greater than one we shared
together and finding it within myself.

- more self-love III

You stayed idle in
the middle of still waters
all this time
and by avoiding the waves
you never really got anywhere.

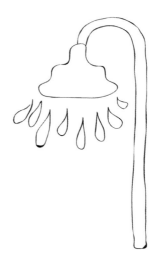

You cannot get over
somebody,
but you can
take a shower.

Jared Singer

As the gates of heaven opens its arms to you,
I hope they are as welcoming as your smile.
I hope that you'll finally be reunited with Lolo.
I hope that you'll be able to walk properly again.
I hope that you'll be up there in peace.
Where there is no pain but joy.
Where there is no frustration but clarity.
Where there is no sadness but the happiness I bitterly wish I could be sharing with you.

- thank you for everything

Growing up,
speaking to my Lola was not easy,
but a common language my
Lola and I shared
was food.

There is no other type of love than the
love provided by your grandmother filling
you up with copious amounts of food.
It is like Santa only coming to one house
and giving one child all the presents.
It's the feeling you get when you sit by
a bonfire because of the warmth and
comfort it provides.
It is as if all the small joys in life came
together and wrapped itself up into a
bundle.
No love can compare to the love I taste in
your food, Lola.
When I eat your food,
it hugs my taste buds,
reminding me of all the

goods things in this world.

. . .

The flavours mingle in perfect harmony
making me feel safe.
The textures so perfect,
it is within its own realm of decadence
that it only affirms my existence.
Only you can give that type of love, Lola.
I know you're happy up there, somewhere,
but
God and I have an odd relationship...
If He were to answer only one prayer of
mine,
it would be to share an eternity of meals
with you someday.

- I'll miss you forever

The world was your oyster
And through conquering this life
Heaven is now your everlasting
Milky Way

- she is everywhere

These moments may be sour
These moments may be sweet
Relish all what you can swallow
and savour what you eat
But never settle with the bitterness of
defeat

- pineapple

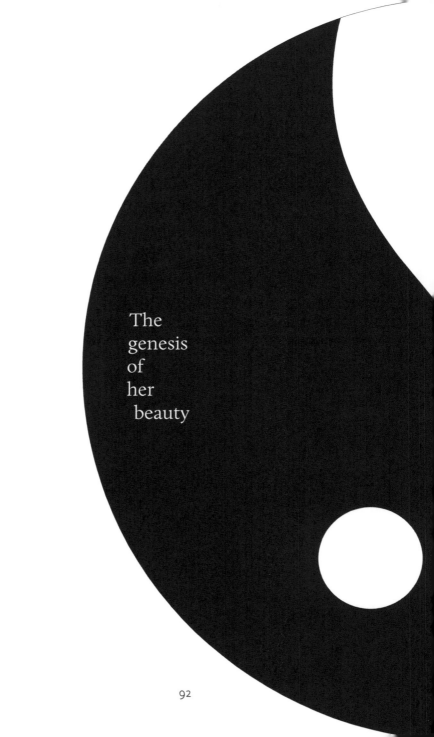

The
genesis
of
her
 beauty

To the
girl I'm deeply
infatuated
with in
the bakery
department
in my local
grocery

On the first day,
God planted the seeds to her body,
every limb,
curve and organ,
blooming and coming together,
bearing fruits to deserts of olive
undertones with trails leading to two
oases resembling her eyes
and when you dip your feet in,
you'll find yourself suddenly submerged
into a vast world of wonderment you
never knew you wanted to be lost in.

There was evening,
and there
was morning,

The second day.
God gave her the most gracefully alluring
hair,
naturally unruffling itself,
flowing down like a calm waterfall you
don't have to hear in order to experience
serenity.

There was evening,
and there
was morning,

The third day.
God said, "let there be light",
giving her smile the ability to radiate an
entire room,
with teeth that form a perfectly aligned
constellation and have everyone
hypnotized,
never having to look through a magnified
scope
to understand how illuminating a star is
when they see one.

There was evening,
and there
was morning,

The fourth day.
God gave her the voice of an angel,
providing the feeling of when you hear
Whitney hit the "AND I" part in 'I will
always love you,'
giving you chills,
making you abruptly good at doing the
shimmy,
and her laugh,
possessing the ability to echo through
crowds and bless those ears as they stop
to grasp how a human has the voice
of a thousand celestial choirs singing
Hallelujah.

There was evening,
and there
was morning,

The fifth day.
God gave the ability for every living
being to faint...
The energy she provides is
unequivocal to anyone or
anything,
slowly evolving into the goddess of
overwhelming beauty,
organically condensing the air
around her
and wearing it thin through her
natural aura,
making you have to almost pass
out because only she can take your
breath away like that.

There was evening,
and there
was morning,

The sixth day.
God gave every living creature
perfect vision
so not one organism with eyes
would have to take a look at her a
second time to
assure that she is so. Fucking.
Beautiful.

There was evening,
and there
was morning,

The seventh and final day.
And on this last day, God rests.
As life on earth came to be,
He didn't realize he had
unintentionally created a mortal
human Venus...
And on that last day,
this creation of His
brought him down to Earth
for he couldn't help himself for a
small moment of
impermanent mortality
and said,

"God damn."

I tell her,
"This introduction is long
overdue."

She says,
"It really is."

I've fallen for many beautiful
people in passing
They've moved in paces remote from me
Or in directions I've been too
afraid to follow
But I've stayed stagnant for you
I thought that this admiration was only
driven through infatuation but
I've read the familiar blemishes written
across your body
And know that you're anything
but a stranger
to me

When people tell me to be myself...

I can't

I breathe in tempos that can't be followed
And stutter in tongues
my tongue
can't even tongue

I've learned that dopamine is one hell of
a drug the moment she spoke to me the
first time

I felt jitters in my chest with my heart
ironically beating to the beat of staying
alive
because I've never felt more animated
than
these moments
with ice surging through my veins
because of how I'm always stuck frozen in
a stupor of admiration when I see her
looking at me
watching her
EXISTING
in front of me

My hands clench like the stubbornness
I've bolstered through the fear of rejection
amplifying in the back of my mind

My body inflamed of the self-prescribed
arthritis that's kept me from making
advances when I try to walk towards her

My body is running high on nothing but a
crush that's as sweet as the orange fizz
Because the moment
she followed me
back on Instagram
Euphoria overwhelmed me
I wasn't able to sleep that night
The following morning I went into my
7am shift feeling like a million bucks as if
my eye bags were Gucci

• • •

Many a times I wanted to say hi
but when I try to connect
the dots in my head
to try and find the words to say
It paints a portrait of you
each time...
and like all pieces of art
I'm left speechless
through your ever glowing beauty
that
I still can't fathom

- Slowly daring me

She's an enchantress in red
Despite wearing the devil
on her body
She's an angel in her
rebellious state
And I've never been more bewitched by a
soul so divine with a heart blemished of
scars drenched in her imperfections
'Cause my god
Just looking at her

It almost feels like a sin

- ilysb

"Tell people how you feel"
she says

Well here you go.

My lungs are a bank vault of breaths that
hold a finite amount of words I wish I
could've shared more in conversation
with you
But
You make me weak
And I relentlessly gasp all that I can
withdraw carelessly
I'm trying my best to solely avoid all that I
can puff and pant when you're around me
You're like a luxury I voluntarily relish
when I luckily have the opportunity to
test drive my disposition on you
Because you make elegance look so
elementary

. . .

So believe me when I say
That I am cycling through my gruelling
vocabulary
That I am trying to express idioms that I
cannot phrase accordingly
That I am trying to make sure that my
tongue would stop slipping onto the
crevices of my chapped lips out of being
sprung on worry

You always take the words out of my
mouth as if I have the insurance to afford
a speech therapist

- at a loss for words

...I know it's rude to leave
your messes for someone else,
but consider also that I'm a mess,
and I make people deal with me
constantly.

Neil Hilborn

Before I let someone else love me...
I can sing along to a lot of Beyoncé songs
but I don't know the titles to her songs.
Yes I'm Asian
and my eyes are fairly bigger
than the average Asian,
so don't be fooled by my Spanish last
name
or my ability to cook pasta
better than a stir fry.
Red is my favourite colour because I
thought the red ranger was the coolest of
the power rangers.
I also have a wide range of sweaters you
can steal,
from oversized pullovers that will make
you feel like a bean bag to
concert sweaters ranging from all genres
to make it look like you're really cultured.
I'm not an alcoholic
but I like beer and liquor
and anything that possesses the ability to
numb my emotions during times of dire
stress and anxiety

and don't be fooled by my confidence
when I'm drunk,
I may be 5'7 but my 6'3 personality takes
over sometimes and isn't fazed by the
insults or rejection
it endures.
I genuinely believe die hard is a wonderful
Christmas movie.
I also like a lot of RNB
and just know I listen to a lot of sad songs
but I'm not always a
sad person,
I'm just a person who happens to like
songs that are sad.
Also, I won't be triggered if you put milk
before your cereal
just because I put cereal before
my milk,
and I might still love you just as much as
I did moments before you hypothetically
poured
that milk first
but... it's okay to be wrong.

· · ·

Before I let someone else love me,
I don't want to scare you but I have this
thing called hyperhidrosis.
Basically if you hold my hand, you may
encounter endless tsunamis creeping into
the cracks of your palms, so I apologize in
advance because I can't help it.
If I refrain from holding your hand
just know that it's not you,
it's me.
But as much as I'd love to hold
your hand at all times,
I don't want you to get washed away by
it after a while because sometimes it gets
triggered when
my mind tingles of paranoia
or by pure excitement if I get a text from
you.

Before I let someone else love me,
I hope you wouldn't mind but
are comforted of the silence I display
sometimes.
My anxieties have anxieties
and I'm sick and tired of always being sick
and tired.
I'm a fairly introverted individual.
I'll need space to recollect my thoughts
and time to keep it intact.
My heart is made up of broken glass
that's barely held together by the amount
of times it's been screwed.
My mind is an endless jigsaw that's pieces
do not possess any straight edges to form
a picture and accumulates more pieces
over time that continue to paint a certain
type of chaos Picasso wouldn't have even
thought of
because in days when I feel less alive than
others,
when I should be counting sheep,
I'm counting on finding reasons in
wanting to do so
and not let go of myself each time.

• • •

I want to assure you that I am not perfect.
I am the furthest star that can be grasped
across the entire universe
and infinity is all I've seemed to ever know
because sometimes the black holes in my
head
are never ending voids of disparities
between
a beautiful galaxy
or cosmic blasts that spontaneously
happen
a little too often.

Before I let someone else love me,
Let me know what keeps you up at night
and I'll take you to Neverland.
Tell me all your insecurities and I'll teach
you how to love yourself.
Lay out all your problems on the table and
I'll help you turn them.
For every time you fall,
I'll be the rock that grounds you
and the pillar that holds you up.
For every time you cry,
we will swim through every

waterfall together until we reach the
shores of nirvana.
Because before I let someone else love me,
I want to assure you that I am not looking
for perfection,
nor am I looking for anything easy.

I'll walk over countless moons to solely
give you the solitude you need to keep on
dancing
and I'll keep loving you naked beyond
your skin.

I'm just waiting for someone who can
look at my soul without those rose tinted
glasses
and choose to uphold this inconvenient
heart,
showing me the
yellow brick road
to a house we can
someday,
call home.

- solely for you

A big thank you to Victoria for being the anchor of this book and providing her expertise in designing the layout and format of the book. Thank you to Alice and Victoria for bringing life to the words I have written with their beautiful illustrations. To those who have listened, critiqued and helped along my journey, I am extremely thankful for your time. Thank you to everyone in my life inspiring me in some way whether it was big or small, your presence is the foundation of all that I have written.